LINDA

True Worship

G000147125

Praising God through a Crisis:

How to Prepare, Survive and Thrive

When Tough Times Hit

Copyright © 2014 Jerry Kuzma

Published by

Perissos Media

www.PerissosMedia.com

ISBN:0992667739

ISBN-13:9780992667733

For a FREE audio sample from this series to share with family or friends, please send them to:

www.MyBookSample.com/worship

CONTENTS

INTRODUCTION

"OH NO!!!"

…or…

"I praise You Jesus!"

When a crisis hits—no matter what form it takes, you have a choice to make. You alone have the power to choose what comes out of your mouth, how you act and how you react to the news.

This is true during the first minute, the first hour and the first day.

Your emotions can take a wild leap, your body tenses up, and everything inside you tries to panic.

How are you going to respond?

More importantly, what can you do to PREPARE YOURSELF, so that you can make it through the crisis?

This vital book is designed to not only instruct you, but also to train you how to PREPARE, SURVIVE and THRIVE in the midst of the battering storms of life—all from a solid, reliable Bible perspective, using PRAISE AND WORSHIP as the main vehicle to make it through the crisis.

I am going to train you how to anchor yourself in the person of God's Messiah, Jesus (or 'Yeshua' in Hebrew). I am also going to show you the vital scriptures that you need to turn 'shock' into peace and 'paralysis' into scriptural action...while you build your personal relationship with the Lord God Himself.

We are going to look at the following areas:

- What a crisis is, and what forms it can take

- How bad news, tragedy and crisis affect your emotions—and how to keep them under control through the wind and waves of the storm

- The key verses and scriptural principles that you need to feed on and build into your personal walk with God

- The absolutely ESSENTIAL part that

praise and worship plays in this whole process

- Why preparing yourself with these scriptures is NOT the same as INVITING trouble or DOUBTING God's protection and provision

- The ONE, CRUCIAL SENTENCE that can carry you through any type of trouble—and, of course, it is based on Scripture

- Why you need to assemble a "First Aid Kit" of praise and worship in your lifestyle, so that you can reach for it in the event of an emergency

- What to do and how to pray—step-by-step—when a crisis hits (place a BOOKMARK in chapter 9!)

- What you can do to support others during their own crisis

Is this book born out of personal experience?

Yes, absolutely.

I have lived through a number of crises, using these very same scriptural principles and examples. I have learned to PREPARE, to SURVIVE and to THRIVE through the storms—while growing closer to God Almighty and His Messiah, Jesus of Nazareth, through the process.

Now, I want to help you to do the same.

If you are ready for truly life-changing training and experience, then let's get started...with a look at what a crisis is.

1. WHAT IS A CRISIS?

First of all, let's define the word 'crisis', so that we can put this whole topic in proper context and also understand what we are going to be talking about.

The dictionary definition of a 'crisis' is this:

1. a stage in a sequence of events at which the trend of all future events, especially for better or for worse, is determined; turning point.

2. a condition of instability or danger, as in social, economic, political, or international affairs, leading to a decisive change.

3. a dramatic emotional or circumstantial upheaval in a person's life.

4. the point in the course of a serious disease at which a decisive change occurs, leading either to recovery or to death.

Now when I think about a crisis, it can fall into a number of different categories. There is the type of crisis that is unexpected, which comes completely out of the blue. You did not know that it was going to take place, and you are left, having to deal with the shock or trauma of it ON TOP OF the actual event itself.

This can take the form of bad news or an

accident, or something bad that happens to one of your loved ones, the place where you work, or the place where you live. Those are the type of things that happen in a completely unexpected way—it certainly brings a crisis situation into your life.

Another type of crisis is where a situation that you are currently dealing with SUDDENLY takes a turn for the worse.

It could be a situation where you are caring for a sick or elderly loved one and their condition suddenly deteriorates.

It could also be a situation where you are dealing with an ongoing stressful situation at work or church, and then something happens to inject a new level of intensity to the stress (that sounds familiar, doesn't it?).

In the second set of examples, you are dealing with circumstances which are not unknown to you or completely unexpected—it is something that is already happening and having an effect in your life. It simply takes on a sudden shift, going from challenging or difficult to TRAUMATIC.

It suddenly starts to affect both your life and other people's lives in a greater, more intense way...and you need help FAST.

In either case, it can have a MASSIVE effect on your life...and you need to know how to survive the initial shock and thrive in the midst of it.

2. TYPES OF CRISIS

Some of the types of crisis that you may experience are these.

Physical—primarily this is a trauma that involves your own body, but it can also be your surroundings, in terms of where you live or work or the vehicle you travel in.

With your physical body, if you have an accident or you endure an event that affects your physical health, you can have a crisis on your hands that is impossible to ignore—it is not something imaginary.

If you are a driver, whether for an employer or for your own benefit—and you break your leg—that is an event that affects your whole life.

It is not simply a physical injury…and it can lead to a crisis situation.

Other crises can affect your physical surroundings, such as storm damage to your house or place of work. When you no longer have a roof over your head, it changes your life in an instant.

Unexpected, traumatic events that alter your life may not happen very often, but they certainly offer you a choice in how you are going to react or respond to them.

Mental—mental crises can take a number of forms, and each one of these can have a drastic effect on your life.

Of course, there are going to be varying degrees of intensity or differences in effect on yourself or your loved ones…and no two lives are the same. Each situation for each person is going to be different.

A mental crisis could occur like this: a person that you work with that blows up at you, loses their temper or harasses you without notice. It could also involve family problems that happen all of a sudden, putting huge amounts of stress on you personally.

You may have a deadline at work or school that is quickly approaching, and it puts strain on your brain. You may have left your tax return to the last minute, and you are struggling to get it done on time to avoid a penalty. There are only 3 hours left to submit your taxes, and you still need 8 hours to get them prepared. Have you been there? I know that I have…

We have all been in that situation. Whether through laziness or procrastination you put something off until the pressure builds and then—boom. You have a crisis on your hands…one that probably could have been avoided with a little bit of organization and forward planning.

Certainly, dealing with children or the elderly, or if you have a loved one who has special needs, these situations can bring mental stress and unforeseen trauma into your life. We love the people—it is just the pressure that can be difficult to deal with. Isn't that right?

How are you doing with this list? Are you finding your story among these examples? There are people who have NOT gone through these types of traumatic events, so let's go through some other kinds of crisis.

Emotional—in the emotional area of life, we can all be vulnerable to a crisis happening from time to time. An emotional crisis can take the form of a breakdown in a relationship with spouse or loved ones, or enduring harassment at work or school, or simply when physical and mental strain starts to get to you.

Physical and mental factors start to wear you down until they affect you emotionally—how you feel about yourself, weeping in private, or feeling like you want to scream at the top of your lungs. It didn't start out in the emotional level, but it reaches the deep parts of you—and you need to do something about it so that you can function normally in life.

An emotional crisis can occur inside yourself, in your own self-worth or self-esteem, bringing you to a crisis point without anyone else involved.

You might have blamed yourself entirely, since there was no one else to blame for the crisis.

There are many wounds that people do not reveal to others...but those are the ones that Jesus wants to heal the most. (That is why we are going to learn how to praise Him IN THE MIDST of the crisis, so that He can move in the midst of your situation.)

When loved ones pass on, you can get hit with a flood of emotions, on top of all the practical factors that have to be dealt with at that crucial time.

Before we go on, I want to encourage you that regardless of what crisis you have already been through or are currently dealing with, GOD HAS A WAY OF BRINGING YOU THROUGH IT!

Let's not go through a long list of trouble and say how bad things are and how devastating it is. You need to know that there is a way to contain your emotions and to receive God's help and wisdom in the midst of your trouble and to make it through to the other side. God Almighty, the God of Abraham, Isaac and Jacob, can make a way in the wilderness for you, if you turn to Him and praise Him in the midst of your trouble.

There are just a few more points that I need to make on this topic.

Other types of crisis—spiritual crises can occur in your own personal walk with God as well. These include peer pressure, temptation, or even the ordinary challenges of the Christian life.

You may also have to face strong-willed believers who try their hardest to put you in your place and pressure you to believe as they do (even though Isaiah 55:12 says, "...you shall go out with joy, and **be led forth with peace**...", not by force).

There is also the possibility of dealing with a crisis involving the spiritual or demonic realms of life—though we are not able to cover that within the scope of this book. However, listen to this: BIBLICAL PRAISE AND WORSHIP are two of your most powerful weapons against the enemy. If you can sing, you can win in those spiritual battles.

As mentioned previously, personal relationships have the potential to bring crisis into your life, even in the midst of joy and happiness in those relationships.

Why? It is simply because human beings are involved, with all their quirks and pre-conceived ideas and emotional baggage and bad reactions—you can experience a host of emotions in any given 24-hour period.

If that is not enough to cover in this chapter, the whole area of financial crises can affect and be linked to the entire list above. Yes, some financial problems occur because of our own mismanagement or bad choices, but often these types of crisis just 'happen' to you (such as when your employer suddenly goes out of business).

This is one area where you DEFINITELY need to know how to praise God in the midst of the trouble.

HERE is one over-riding factor in these traumatic events, not matter what it is that you are facing: it all tries to affect your emotions in such a way that you feel overwhelmed…and you don't know how to handle it.

As we look at the emotional effects in this next chapter, remember that we are learning about this so that we can OVERCOME THE

OVERWHELM and invite the Lord to BRING US THROUGH the storm.

Ready to move on? Let's go.

3. HOW A CRISIS AFFECTS YOUR EMOTIONS

No matter what type of crisis you face, it tends to have a similar impact on your emotions.

You may have to deal with stress, anxiety, anger, confusion, depression, panic, weeping, rage, numbness or fighting with family members. You could also be dealing with a number of those emotions each day.

One of the most common responses is TOTAL PARALYSIS—where you simply just shut down and do nothing at all. It is a critical state to be in, but you can relate to that, can't you?

It all paints a picture of this: your emotions are shouting louder than any other part of you, stealing your attention and distracting you from the very things that will bring RELIEF in the middle of the situation.

The one, reliable source of relief in your crisis situation is GOD ALMIGHTY Himself.

To be clear, I am not talking about some generic god-like figure, or whatever deity that you choose to serve. I am talking about the God of the Bible—the God of Israel— and His Messiah as revealed in the Hebrew

24

Scriptures, Yeshua the Messiah, Jesus of Nazareth.

Through <u>specific</u> verses in His book, He is able to intervene in the midst of your situation and bring relief, peace, wisdom and joy—no matter what you are facing.

However, when tough times hit you, when a crisis jumps up and demands your attention and tries to override your emotions, it can be difficult to FOCUS on God and REACH for the verses that will bring you through the battle.

For instance, when a huge, unexpected bill comes in and you experience stress and panic, the most common response is for your mind to start racing. You try to work out what money you can take from your budget to fix the problem—even if you have no way to pay the entire amount. Your mind believes that it must be able to solve the problem, one way or another.

Your MIND thinks that it can figure it out, so it races in to take control…but it is all based on the panic that comes from not knowing how to solve the problem.

Unless you PREPARE yourself and TRAIN your brain with God's word, it could take hours or days or weeks before you stop and ask God for help.

Think about a movie cinema. If someone shouts "FIRE!", panic could easily set in if the cinema staff do not intervene, calming and directing the movie viewers to safety.

Left to your own human emotions, nothing good can come of it, because your mind isn't as bulletproof or infallible as it thinks that it is.

You need help, and you need it fast.

You need peace, you need wisdom to know what to do, you need support from beyond your own resources, and you need hope for a good outcome.

God, through His Word, is the only reliable source for all those things.

So, how do we keep our emotions under control, so that we can reach out to the Lord during crisis situations?

That is what we are going to look at now, in the next chapter.

4. KEEPING YOUR EMOTIONS UNDER CONTROL

When tough times occur or bad news reaches you, it can hit both your mind and your emotions at the same time.

It can feel overwhelming in that split second...but God is smart; He has given us a scripture to cover that particular situation...one that has brought me through plenty of challenging situations and stressful circumstances.

This one verse, committed to memory and made a part of your daily life, will absolutely ANCHOR your emotions in the event of any crisis occurring.

"[The righteous man] shall not be afraid of

evil tidings: his heart is fixed, trusting in the LORD." ~ Psalm 112:7 KJV

The Modern King James Version translates it this way:

"He shall not be afraid of bad news; his heart is fixed, trusting in [the Lord]."

You see? God has already covered this area in His Word. Believe me, it is a good thing that He has.

In the context of verse 1, God is talking about the man who greatly delights in His commandments...the person who loves God's word and is in right relationship with Him.

Please notice that it does NOT say that you will never hear bad news or that crisis or challenges will never touch your life.

Even a crisis that occurs to a loved one can affect you as deeply as if it happened to you yourself.

When bad news reaches your ears, when evil tidings or any other crisis situation springs into your life, you have a verse that helps you to grab onto GOD HIMSELF and FIX yourself to Him.

Look again at that verse. Stop long enough to take it all in, and THINK about what it says.

"He will not fear evil tidings." He will not be afraid of bad news. Why?

Is he fearless because he is blind or deaf to the news, or because he is stupid or lazy? No.

"...his heart is FIXED, trusting in the Lord."

Another version translates that word as "steadfast", but it paints the same picture.

The Hebrew word there is "kûn", a primary root which the Strong's Dictionary defines as "to set up, establish, fix, prepare, apply, fasten, be fitted, be fixed, to ordain, to set in order, to perfect, to prepare or make ready." There is a solidity to this word.

It paints a picture of a heart that is firmly FASTENED or ANCHORED to the Lord and to His character.

The winds may blow, the storm may surge, but this man's heart is <u>welded and bolted</u> onto the God of Israel and His promises.

His heart is FIXED, permanently attached, no matter what may try to move him.

Do you see the conflict in that verse?

Fear is trying to grip this man, not because of some imaginary problem or mental deficiency, but because of a real live situation that is trying to overwhelm him—all of a sudden.

Fear is battling against his trust in the living God, trying to sweep him out to sea. However, this man has done something to PREPARE himself ahead of time, before the bad news arrives.

"…his heart is fixed…"

Look at it. WHO has done the "fixing"?

The man himself has.

He has decided to take a stance that defies the fear and bad news.

He has said in his heart (and probably out

loud):

"I—WILL—TRUST—THE—LORD, NO MATTER WHAT HAPPENS IN MY LIFE!"

He himself has "fixed" his trust in the character of the Lord, and his emotions must follow suit.

His body, his mind and his human spirit are pulling together to bring his emotions under control.

"**I—WILL**—TRUST—THE—LORD". He has made his choice, and he has fixed his heart to the promise of Almighty God.

Burn this into your mind, and let the Lord use it to FIX your heart to Him:

"I—WILL—TRUST—THE—LORD, NO

MATTER WHAT HAPPENS IN MY LIFE!"

Now, we need to look at specific verses that will build you up in your trust—your faith—in His character, because "...faith comes by hearing and hearing from the Word of God" (Romans 10:17).

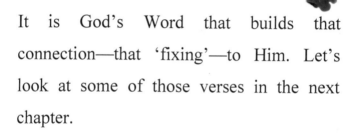

It is God's Word that builds that connection—that 'fixing'—to Him. Let's look at some of those verses in the next chapter.

5. KEY VERSES AND PRINCIPLES

To be blunt, it is God's Word ALONE that builds that connection, that FIXES you heart to Him in times of crisis.

It is specific verses that do this…

…and it is best to FIX your heart to Him with His promises ahead of time.

Let's explore some of the key principles in doing this, as well as the key verses that they are built upon.

God Is Bigger

"But what if my house just burned down?"

Of course, that is a major disaster, and it is a huge crisis to happen to you and your family. However, God is BIGGER than your house.

Broken marriage? God is bigger than your marriage or its break-up.

This is one of the primary foundations of our study of this topic today. The crisis tries to tell you that IT is bigger, but the Bible tells you that God is BIGGER than the crisis.

Remember this verse from the Psalms:

"The floods have lifted up, O Lord, the floods have lifted up their voice; the floods lift up their waves. **The LORD on high is**

mightier than the noise of many waters, yes, than the mighty waves of the sea." Psalm 93:3-4

The Lord HIMSELF is mightier than the crashing waves—not a church, not a minister, not your family or friends. It is the Lord and His merciful, heroic character that is mightier than any crisis.

When you firmly fix yourself to the One, True, BIG God, you can survive anything that could possibly happen to you. He is BIGGER than it all.

Jesus' Greatest Commandment

Most Christians do not even know or recognize that Jesus made this crucial statement in Matthew's gospel, nor do they realize how vital it is to their life in God.

One of the specialists in the Torah (the Hebrew Scriptures) asks Jesus a very important question.

"Master, which is the great commandment in the law? Jesus said unto him, **'Thou shalt love the Lord thy God with all thy heart, and with all thy soul, and with all thy mind.'** This is the first and <u>GREATEST</u> commandment." ~ Matthew 22:36-38

Did Jesus just make up that response? Of course not. He was quoting the "Shema", from the Torah itself, in Deuteronomy 6:5:

"Hear ['Shema' in Hebrew], O Israel: The Lord our God is one Lord: And you shall love the LORD your God with all your heart, and with all your soul, and with all your might. And these words, which I command you this day, shall be <u>in your</u>

40

heart...." ~ Deuteronomy 6:4-6

This one verse is so central to the lives of the Jewish people, those who love the Lord and love His Word...and Jesus quotes it as the GREATEST COMMANDMENT.

It is also the pre-eminent scripture on praise and worship, as it paints a picture of a believer who loves the Lord with every fibre of his being—and expresses that love through praise, worship and everyday life.

In my own opinion, we have seriously neglected Jesus' words regarding the Shema...and so we have cut ourselves off from the power in that part of scripture.

It is what Jesus Himself calls the GREATEST commandment in the whole book!

I think that it is funny—and tragic—that we all say that we love Jesus, that we want to follow Jesus and imitate Jesus, yet we do not want to know about His greatest commandment.

In my 27+ years of being a Christian, I have never heard any pastor or teacher say, "The Shema is Jesus' greatest commandment...and you need to learn it, memorize it and LIVE IT!"

Well, let's start doing it right now.

The Shema is central to the Jewish heart because it is central to the heart of God Himself...and so it was central to the heart of Jesus.

Therefore, it should be central to your heart and mine as well.

"…you shall love the LORD your God with all your <u>heart</u>, and with all your <u>soul</u>, and with all your <u>might</u>."

So how does this apply to praising God through a crisis?

Please notice the word 'soul' in the Shema.

"…love the LORD your God with all your… soul…"

Your soul is generally defined as you mind, your willpower and your emotions.

God wants our emotions to worship Him and to be submitted to His lordship. He wants our emotions to be FIXED in submission to Him.

When we make Him Lord over our emotions, when we declare and remember that He is God on the throne—and our emotions are NOT—we get into the place of humility before Him.

"No matter what I face, Lord, you are greater than it all—greater than my crisis, greater than my feelings about it."

[Now would be a good time to stop reading for a moment and pray that out to the Lord—right now. Go ahead…I'll wait till you are done…]

"No matter what I face, Lord, you are greater than it all—greater than my crisis, greater than my feelings about it…

AND………..I will worship You, Lord, no matter what happens!"

Can you see why that scripture is so vital? Do you see how it paints a picture of your life, loving Him, praising Him, serving Him with all that you are and all that you have?

It flows right into our next key principle...and the verse that I have spoken and sung for decades—one that has become a cornerstone of my own personal worship life.

Praise God Throughout Your Day, Throughout Your Life

Here it is...Psalm 34:1.

Our wonderful children have heard me quote this verse to them countless times, because they need it as much as we do as parents.

"I will bless the LORD at all times: His praise shall continually be in my mouth." ~ Psalm 34:1

There is so much meat, so much depth in this short verse, but it is too easy to assume what it means and just brush it off—and miss the power that God has poured into this verse.

Let's dig into it, so that God can establish something powerful into your life and equip you for any challenges that happen in your life.

The verse starts off with the phrase "I will...."

Yes, "I will." This is all about your willpower, your choice, your exercising your strength of character to open your mouth and begin to praise God. This single two-word phrase is one of the most powerful phrases that can come out of your lips, either for good or for evil.

You know that God gave Adam the freedom of choice in the Garden of Eden...He did NOT make him a robot.

In essence, God said to Adam, "You can eat this, or this, or this, but son, do not eat this one over here. I am leaving that one in the garden, and I am not making it invisible.

You are going to see that tree...and every time you see it, you are going to have to make the CHOICE to avoid it [Kuzma paraphrase]."

Adam had to exercise his God-given power of choice in his daily life...and so do you.

Your power of choice is a potent thing, and God wants you to use it to make GOOD choices—especially when you are under pressure.

Let's go back to Psalm 34:1 and take another look at this verse.

"I will bless the Lord at all times; His praise shall continually be in my mouth."

When the psalmist tells us this, he is giving his own life as an example. "I—myself—will bless the Lord...." This is my own responsibility, my own choice, my personal decision that no one can take away from me.

(I also cannot blame anyone else if I do NOT do this verse.....ouch!)

Listen to this: your own personal decision to bless and praise the Lord, based on scripture, in the middle of every situation, is the SINGLE, MOST POTENT DECISION that you can make as a believer.

Why can I make that statement? It is because…to ACT on God's Word in faith, and to praise Him with all your heart when you are under fire, is extremely pleasing to the Lord Himself. He loves it…and he will STRONGLY SUPPORT YOU when you do it!

Time for another one of my favorite verses:

"For the eyes of the LORD move to and fro throughout the earth, that He might strongly support those whose heart is completely His." ~ 2 Chronicles 16:9a

God is LOOKING for someone who worships Him with their whole heart.

If that is you—if your heart is completely His—then He is LOOKING to strongly support you.

Now that you know that verse, it should make you want to jump and shout and praise God with all your heart…and get ready for Him to move mightily in your situation!

One quick warning though, if you are in the middle of a crisis situation: your praise and worship had better be biblically based, or God will not be able to help you. Let's look at that issue in the next chapter.

6. YOUR PRAISE MUST BE BIBLICALLY BASED

If you are in a crisis situation, it is very easy to gripe, complain or just cry and cry. Every one of your emotions could take turns, all trying to take the helm of your life.

Since you desperately need the Lord's help at that moment, you must make sure that you are coming to Him in faith, based on His Word.

Why?

"The Bible tells me so…" (or rather, these verses tell me so).

"But without faith, it is impossible to please Him…" (Hebrews 11:6a) and "…faith comes by hearing and hearing from the word of God." (Romans 10:17).

So, we can only please God with faith that is firmly based on His own Word, as revealed in the Bible.

No matter how your emotions feel, <u>God requires biblical faith</u>—EVEN when you are in a crisis situation.

Don't you see? When a crisis hits, you have a choice to make. Your emotions want to dictate your response.

God wants your biblical faith to dictate your response.

What is your best response—your only response?

Here is your answer: You must grab hold of SPECIFIC verses from God's Word, and begin to <u>say them</u>, <u>believe them</u> and <u>sing them</u>, until you come through your crisis.

Your emotions have to be set aside, on purpose, so that you can praise God with His Word...and invite Him into your situation.

God responds to His own word, when you believe it and say or SING it back to Him...

...and there is no better time than RIGHT NOW!

7. THE ONE CRUCIAL SENTENCE THAT WILL CARRY YOUR THROUGH

If there is one, single thought...one verse...one principle that I would love to inject into your head and heart—in order to carry you through even the worst crisis imaginable, it would be this one.

We have mentioned this verse before, but we cannot get enough of this verse into our hearts.

Why?

The answer is simple: you need a very strong and sound ANCHOR to hold your thoughts and emotions in place when the winds start to rock your boat.

This one verse has been on my lips during hard times more than any other.

Once again, look with me at **Psalm 34:1.**

"I WILL bless the Lord at ALL TIMES; His praise shall CONTINUALLY be in my MOUTH."

If you say this, and say this, and say this, until you completely commit it to memory and make it a part of you, God Himself will use this verse to pull you through the hardest challenges.

He loves this verse…because He wrote it.

He wrote it for YOU.

"I will bless the Lord at ALL times." That means good times, challenging times, stressful times, happy and joyous times, times of battle, times of finally breaking through—ALL TIMES.

This is to become a part of your life.

My friend, you were created to worship God…that is why He put His own breath into you…so that you could use it to sing back to Him.

Does God sing? Yes, of course He does. Look at this:

"You are my hiding place; You shall preserve me from trouble; You shall circle

[or surround] me with songs of deliverance."
~ Psalm 32:7

God Himself sings over you with songs of deliverance...surrounding you with His songs...because He wants you to come through your trial and come closer to Him.

"I will bless the Lord at all times." You will notice that He did NOT use the words GRIPE, MOAN, COMPLAIN or REHEARSE-HOW-BAD-IT-IS. He said to BLESS HIM. Praise Him.

Tell Him how great and mighty He is, no matter what situation you find yourself in.

Proclaim His goodness.

Shout out loud how faithful He is.

Tell your soul: "Soul, you have a thousand

reasons to praise the Lord, so start to praise right now."

My eldest child was diagnosed as Special Needs many years ago…a condition that we are trusting God for breakthrough in.

He loves the Lord with all his heart, and he knows the Bible well.

I tell him this verse quite often, and I use that sentence above all the time with him.

"Son, you have a THOUSAND reasons to praise the Lord. You need to praise Him for WHO YOU ARE and WHAT YOU HAVE, instead of complaining about WHO YOU ARE NOT and WHAT YOU DO NOT HAVE.

I need to do the same…and so do you.

If you are feeling challenged, start to praise God for the air that you are breathing. It reminds me of a thought that a friend sent me one day, and I shared it on social media:

"You should praise God for OXYGEN; you have been breathing it AT NO CHARGE for your entire life!!"

Yes, I have breath, and so do you...but that reminds me of another verse:

"Let everything that has breath PRAISE the Lord!" ~ Psalm 150:6

That includes me, so I am going to act on that verse and praise Him right now...as long as I am breathing.

THAT is why we need to develop the HABIT of praising God in the midst of every situation—to prepare yourself and be ready for anything that life throws at us, and to THRIVE in the midst of it!

This idea of preparing yourself ahead of time is the topic of our next chapter…and it is one of the most practical—and somewhat controversial—topics in this book. Let's turn the page and get started….

8. BUILDING A 'FIRST AID KIT' OF PRAISE AND WORSHIP

Why do you need to learn to praise God in every situation, at all times, at any time of the day or night?

If for no other reason than sheer obedience, it is simply to develop the habit of a praising lifestyle—for times when you REALLY NEED to praise Him and get Him involved in your challenging situation.

Tonight, I was teaching and training two of our teens to do just that...to praise God out loud, on the spot.

Was it a challenge for them to do this OUT LOUD?

Yes...obviously.

Did they do it?

Yes, reluctantly.

I told them that they need to prepare themselves, so that they know how to praise God during a crisis, so that they know what to do ahead of time.

YOU need to do the same, for the very same reason.

I know that this might be a challenging principle to learn, especially because most

Bible-based churches do NOT teach this to their congregations.

Not just a lack of teaching, but there is a serious lack of hands-on training in this area.

I am saying this after 25+ years in worship ministry, church board membership, teaching and leadership positions, and being in the pew in a number of churches and fellowships.

I see a great need for believers in Messiah Jesus to be TRAINED in a praising lifestyle, so that their lives aren't shipwrecked if something doesn't go to plan.

So, with that said, let's talk about opening your Bible, digging into God's word and building yourself a praise and worship 'first aid kit'.

"What?"

No, Jimmy, I haven't switched book pages on you...we need to build you a 'first aid kit'.

Well, if you think about the phrase 'first aid kit', you get a picture of a small package or box that you pull out of storage when an emergency arises...isn't that right?

You might have one in your car, in your house, or at your place of employment (your employer will certainly have one or two there, for health and safety reasons).

Now, what do you have inside that kit? You will have bandages, tape, simple medicines, etc.—a collection of different materials and treatments that you can pick from in the event of an emergency.

They are PREPARED AHEAD OF TIME, ready to use if a crisis situation occurs. Those items are always kept clean, dry and ready to use.

The items that you choose from that first aid kit will depend on the NATURE of the crisis that you are treating someone for.

For example, you don't need a small adhesive bandage if your child has fractured his wrist—you may need an elastic bandage and a tourniquet for that particular emergency.

If your child gets a foreign object or particle in his eye, he does not need a tourniquet— sterile eyewash and some sterile pads are needed in that situation.

In the same way, you need to prepare yourself ahead of time with a praise and worship lifestyle—like a first aid kit—in the event of an emergency.

We have already talked about the need for scriptures that 'anchor' your emotions during a crisis, so that your feelings don't take over and start to dictate your behavior at that moment.

Now listen—those scripture verses that we talked about earlier are the key to this principle.

The way that you train yourself to anchor your emotions in the spur of the moment is to PREPARE yourself ahead of time with those verses.

When you spend time in Psalm 34:1 ("I will bless the Lord at all times…"), committing it memory and meditating on it regularly, you begin to make it a CENTRAL part of your walk with the Lord.

You need to build that inside of yourself, making it roll off your tongue as naturally as breathing.

When you make that one verse a part of your daily life, you are essentially storing it away in your own praise and worship 'first aid kit"—ready to call upon whenever needed.

Of course, this same principle can be applied to verses concerning ANY part of your Christian walk. Certainly, you can learn specific verses and make them a part of your life, so that you can stand in faith in the middle of a challenging situation—with your heart and mind ANCHORED to the Lord.

However, I am talking specifically about feeding on verses concerning your praise and worship life—because they are CRUCIAL to your stability and well-being in the midst of a crisis situation.

THAT is why we need to feed on these verses, to build a praise and worship lifestyle, and to assemble a 'first aid kit' of praise ahead of time.

Let me tell you from personal experience— when you make Psalm 34:1 a part of your day and a part of your life, God will be able to draw upon it during your trying times.

Pack that one into your 'first aid kit'.

You may need to write your praise and worship scriptures down on paper or a piece of card, so that you can read them as you recite them.

"Betty, did he just use the word 'recite'?"

"Yes Jimmy, he did."

I know that you may not have had to 'recite' anything since you were in primary school, but it is a great word—and a brilliant principle for committing scriptures to memory.

When we SEE and HEAR and SPEAK those verses, out loud, over and over, our brains build them into the deep parts of our memory. They get super-glued into your memory, so that you can call upon them in the future as you need them.

It worked for your multiplication tables (or it should have), and it works even better when you want to memorize scripture.

As you commit these vital verses to memory, the Lord can bring them up to your conscious mind at the crucial times in your life.

Here is another verse that sheds light on the topic of scripture memorization:

"But the Comforter, who is the Holy Spirit, whom the Father will send in My name, He shall teach you all things, and bring all things to your remembrance, whatsoever I have said unto you." ~ **John 14:26**

Jesus said that the Holy Spirit would bring the Lord's words to your remembrance—

that He would REMIND you of His word. What a powerful promise!

You should stop reading for a moment and thank God that He reminds you of His word!

"Thank you Father that you sent the Holy Spirit to remind me of Your word, and that He will be bringing it back to my mind when I need it most."

Of course, you need to build yourself up in your faith in the areas of holiness, peace, love, healing, provision, protection, and your prayer life.

However, what sets this area of praise and worship apart from the others is that it TOUCHES every other part of your walk with God.

More importantly, your praise and worship

life ANCHORS your head and heart to the Lord, especially in times of trial, trouble or utter crisis.

Shipbuilders do not forge that anchor and chain when they are sailing around on the high seas, do they?

No.

They forge it from hardened steel well before they leave the dock, so that when the need arises to drop that anchor and to rely on its strength and stability, it will hold the ship fast and keep it from being wrecked on the rocks.

Be as wise as a salty old seaman...forge your 'anchor' from the word of God and keep it handy.

Make those verses a part of your daily life—

sing them, sing them, and then sing them again. Make up your own melodies with them. Commit them to memory, and let them roll off your tongue when you are shopping, working, driving or walking Fluffy the dog.

You will be storing them in your own private first aid kit, ready to help you—or someone you love—in a moment of need.

Next, we are going to go over the actual steps that you need to take when a crisis hits. Get ready, because this could literally save your life....

9. YOUR 'FIRST AID KIT' – WHAT TO DO IN A CRISIS, STEP-BY-STEP

We have talk a lot about the circumstances and principles behind praising God through a crisis. Now, we need to go through this, one step at a time.

If you are currently in the middle of a crisis, then this .has now become the most important chapter in this book.

Nothing else matters—you need to get close

to God Almighty through His Word and invite Him into the middle of your situation.

STEP 1. Get yourself right with God

There is, however, ONE prerequisite—ONE essential requirement—to you coming close to the God of the Bible and receiving lasting help from Him.

Do you know what it is?

You must be in a total, sold-out relationship with Him through the sacrifice of His Messiah, Yeshua/Jesus of Nazareth.

I don't know what your background is or what you have or have not been taught about the God of Israel, but there is only ONE way to get to Him. That one way is through His Messiah.

Jesus (or "Yeshua" in Hebrew) is the only man in history that fits the exact biblical description of God's Messiah, as revealed in the Hebrew Scriptures.

He was and is the only way to get close to the God of the whole earth.

If you have never given your life over to God and asked His Messiah to be Lord of your life, then THAT is the first step that you need to take.

You need to do that NOW, before we go through any of the other steps.

(You may have a lot of questions at this point, but you can get help from a local pastor who can guide you through any questions that you have).

Here is a simple, Bible-based prayer that

you can follow. Please read through it a few times until you understand it, and then pray it out loud from your heart, speaking directly to God Himself.

[Even if you already have a relationship with God through Jesus, NOW is the perfect time to get yourself right with Him.]

God of Israel, I believe that you are the one true God, and that you made me with Your own hands. You know me inside and out.

I believe that you sent Yeshua—Jesus—to make a way for me to come close to You and receive all I need from you.

I know that I have sinned over and over again, and that I cannot save myself, no matter how hard that I try.

I believe that Jesus is the one true Messiah,

and that He shed His blood to pay the price for all my sins. He died and rose from the dead to make a way for me, because He loves me with all of His heart.

God, please forgive me of all the sins that I have done up to this point in my life.

Please wash me clean, set me free from every bondage, and help me to praise You and worship You and love You with all of my heart.

Thank you, Lord, for giving me a new life, starting today, through the work of Yeshua—Jesus the Messiah. Amen.

If you understood that and prayed it—and meant it—then God has given you a new life with Him, and He has created an avenue to help you in the midst of your crisis.

STEP 2. Dedicate your mouth to praising God, no matter what happens

KEY VERSE: "I will bless the LORD at all times: His praise shall continually be in my mouth." ~ Psalm 34:1

Say this verse over and over, loud enough for your own ears to hear it. Say the first phrase over and over, and then the second phrase.

"I will bless the Lord at ALL TIMES...good times, bad times, confused times, tired times...at all times, no matter what is happening at this moment."

This is an absolutely VITAL verse, because you use this verse to train your mouth. You are training your mouth, and your brain, to praise God INSTANTLY, whenever something challenging happens. This invites God into your situation right away, and it could save your life in that split second.

"His praise shall CONTINUALLY be in my mouth. I am dedicating my mouth to the Lord of Heaven, because He deserves praise in the middle of EVERY situation."

Your mouth can either help you or hinder you in the midst of this crisis situation— make the quality decision to fill it with PRAISE, no matter what.

STEP 3. Declare that God's WRITTEN WORD will have first place in this situation

KEY VERSE: "Your Word is a lamp unto my feet and a light unto my path." ~ Psalm 119:105

In marked contrast to what your emotions want you to do, you must keep the Scriptures as the focus of your attention.

The Bible is God's written Word, His rule book and His authoritative basis for life on this planet. When you desperately need God's help, that is NOT the time to begin saying and praying a lot of stuff that directly contradicts what He has already written.

In the midst of a crisis, you need to hold fast to His Word—even if you are still learning it for yourself. Tell Him that you are sticking to His Word.

"Almighty God, I am going to hold onto Your Word, because it says that it is a lamp to my feet, and You are going to use it to light my path. Your Word will help me to know what to do in this situation.

I trust You, Father God, and I trust the Word that You have written. I praise You for your Word, and I thank you for using it to help me through this.

STEP 4. Declare that God is MUCH BIGGER than the situation you are facing

KEY VERSE: The LORD on high is mightier than...the mighty waves of the sea." ~ Psalm 93:3-4

Remember that we talked about how the crisis tries to make you feel powerless, and your emotions can go a bit out of control?

Now is the time to use your freshly-dedicated mouth to declare that GOD HIMSELF is in charge of this situation, and that He is bigger and mightier than every part of it.

Begin to tell Him that you trust Him, because He is strong and mighty—and He is on your side!

"God, I praise You because you are mightier than the mighty waves of the sea. You are greater than every living thing on this planet, bigger than every sickness, every debt, every enemy, every accident, every trauma—and I put my whole trust in You.

Nothing in my life is greater than You, and nothing has surprised You or caught you off guard. You are in control of this entire situation. Thank you for making me Your child, and thank you for bringing me through all of this. I praise You with all of my heart."

There is a very real strength that God pours into your heart, into your human spirit, when you praise Him in the midst of challenging circumstances. It is His own strength, empowered by His Holy Spirit, which will gird you up and bring you through.

STEP 5. Submit your emotions to God

KEY VERSES: "...not My will, but Yours, be done." ~ Luke 22:42b

"Surely I have stilled and quieted my soul...." ~ Psalm 131:2a

Right now, your emotions are battling for control, and you must grab ahold of your emotional state and submit it to God. This is a vital step in our 'first aid kit', because your emotions are connected to your brain and your mouth.

When we decide to make Jesus the Lord over our emotions and reactions, we are essentially stopping ourselves from just saying whatever wants to come out of our mouth at the moment.

We are putting a "bridle on our tongue" (James chapter 3), so that we don't offend the Lord, whose help we desperately need.

When we pray the words of Jesus, "…not my will, but Yours, be done," we are putting our willpower under His command. You MUST do this, so that you don't haul off and make some hasty decision that makes matters worse.

You also have to "still and quiet your soul", which means that you need to make a firm decision to TELL your emotions to quiet down, like a mother quiets her children.

You do NOT have to be ruled by your emotions, even if a huge crisis has taken place. With God's help, you can draw on His strength and keep your emotions at bay.

"Father God, right here in the midst of this challenging situation, I decide to place my emotions on Your altar. No matter how I feel, I say to You, 'Not my will, but Yours, be done.' I will do what You say, and I will wait for Your leading.

I ask You to be Lord over my emotions, so that I don't mess things up in the middle of this. You are bigger than my heart, and I trust You with my emotions.

I speak to my mind, my will and my emotions, and I tell you to be still and be quiet. The Lord Himself is in charge of my life.

Thank You God for taking Your place as Lord over my heart. I pray this in the Name of Jesus my Messiah, amen."

STEP 6. Ask God for His peace.

KEY VERSES: "Do not be anxious about anything, but in everything, by <u>prayer</u> and <u>petition</u> with <u>THANKSGIVING</u>, let your <u>requests be made known</u> to God. And the peace of God which passes all understanding shall <u>GUARD your hearts and minds</u> through Messiah Jesus." ~ Philippians 4:6-7

The Bible actually commands us to be anxious/uptight/stressed-out about NOTHING.

Yes, what a challenge, isn't it?

However, if He put it into the Bible, then He has a way to HELP you to do it. In fact, God tells us exactly what to do instead.

That section of Scripture tells us to RESIST worry, instead of embracing it and drinking it in like water.

It tells us to PRAY and MAKE PETITION; in other words, stop and ask God for help.

It says to make THANKSGIVING, which means to start thanking Him for His peace and His help, instead of worrying about it.

Yes, that is one of the BIGGEST parts that praise and worship play in this whole process. Praise Him RIGHT NOW, even before you see and answer or feel one drop of peace flow down onto you.

What will the outcome be? That verse says that our Messiah's peace will GUARD your heart and mind. It will start to protect you from worrying thoughts and all of those "worst-case scenarios" that you brain likes to think up—as long as you CONTINUE to praise Him in the midst of the situation.

His peace will guard your mind. Thank God for His peace!

STEP 7. Ask God for His wisdom.

KEY VERSE: But if any of you lacks wisdom, let him ask of God, Who gives to all liberally and with no reproach, and it shall be given to him. ~ James 1:5

When you are in the middle of a crisis or some other challenging situation, that is the time when you really need God's wisdom. His wisdom is like the background information—the understanding of the bigger picture—that helps you to cope with and overcome the immediate circumstances.

For example, my car broke down recently, leaving us stranded on the side of a road. I got my family home in a taxi, and I had to arrange for my car to be towed to a mechanic.

I was praying for God's help and wisdom regarding the breakdown, and the answer came through an unexpected source some time later: there was a simple bit of maintenance that I had not done, and this was the cause of the car's breakdown.

When we receive God's peace and then ask Him for His wisdom and understanding regarding a crisis situation, He can answer in a number of different ways—but He DOES answer.

Obviously, we are not going to be able to cover the entire subject of hearing from God as revealed in the Bible—that would be a book in itself. However, I do know from Scripture and from experience that God's PEACE and His WISDOM go hand-in-hand.

This verse taught me that principle years ago, and I still rely on it when I need God's wisdom:

"...you shall go out with joy, and be LED FORTH WITH PEACE...." ~ Isaiah 55:12

No matter what direction that the Lord wants to give to you, whether the information is comforting or challenging, He will always wrap His wisdom with His peace, so that you can KNOW that it is Him directing you.

Does that make sense?

Peace is part of His signature, His character, a tell-tale sign of His wisdom and His presence. Even if God had to deliver unwelcome news or blunt facts to you in the midst of your crisis, He would "sign" that memo with His peace, so that you could know that it was from Him.

He leads with peace, so His peace and His direction go together.

Let's pray—using that verse as our guideline.

Father God, I thank You that Your word says that 'I will be led forth with peace', because I am in covenant with You. I thank You for Your peace, and I ask you to lead me and guide me with Your wisdom.

I put my own reasoning and my emotions aside, I still my soul, and I receive your wisdom for this crisis situation. You want me to understand what is happening behind the scenes, in the bigger picture, and You want me to have peace in the midst of it. I thank You Lord, in the name of Jesus.

It is also important—and advisable—to stay connected with other mature believers, who can double-check any impressions or directions that you receive during this time. This is to safeguard you during this emotionally-charged period of time.

Also, it is vitally important to continue THANKING God for His wisdom, even while you are still waiting to hear it or act on it.

STEP 8. Silence your 'enemy'

KEY VERSES: "...Out of the mouth of babes and infants <u>You have perfected praise</u>...." ~ Matthew 21:16b (based on Psalm 8:2)

"Out of the mouth of babes and infants You have ordained strength because of Your enemies, that You might <u>silence the enemy and the avenger</u>." ~ Psalm 8:2

The <u>good</u> news is that God loves you and He wants to help you in the midst of your situation. The <u>bad</u> news is that Satan is currently still on the loose, wanting to wreck your life.

The <u>great</u> news is that you are NOT helpless in this situation.

Again, we could write a few books on the subject of exercising your God-given authority over demon spirits, but others have covered that subject very well.

What you need right now is a clear, biblical strategy for keeping the enemy at bay while you are dealing with the immediate situation.

THAT is where biblical praise and worship comes into play.

According to our two key verses, God has directed believers to give Him whole-hearted praise (simply because He deserves it). However, it also has the ability to also SILENCE the demonic realm who are standing against you.

Why would mature, perfected praise have this effect on your enemies?

It is because whole-hearted, biblical praise

98

invites God Almighty Himself into your situation, and that in itself will send the enemy running.

Whole-hearted, biblical praise and worship also carries God's anointing—His power and glory—so that the enemy gets 'beat up' by the power of God while you are singing away and worship Him!

"In His presence is the fullness of joy." ~ Psalm 16:11

When you invite God into your crisis through biblical praise and worship, and He manifests His presence in the middle of your situation, it produces joy and refreshing— which is the exact opposite of what your enemy wants to inject into your life.

"Let the high praises of God be in their

mouth...to bind their kings with chains and their nobles with iron-bands...." ~ Psalm 149:6,8

Those verses talk about HIGH PRAISE—praising God with ALL of your heart and ALL of your soul and ALL of your mind and ALL of your strength—reaching the HEIGHTS of praising God. It drives your enemy away, because he cannot stand it!

God, right here, right now, I worship You with all of my heart and soul and mind and strength. I give every part of my life to You, so that You can truly be Lord over me.

Use my every breath, every thought, every emotion, and every habit and action to bring praise to Your holy name. I am Yours, Lord. Jesus, be Lord over this situation and over my entire life. Amen"

True worship silences your enemy and invites more of God's presence and power into your crisis. NOW is a good time to start....

STEP 9. Declare God's Word boldly, with passion and confidence

KEY VERSE: "...I watch over My Word to perform it." ~ Jeremiah 1:12b

Basically, God responds to His Word. He is LOOKING for you to pray His Word back to Him. When we take His own words and pray and declare them in the midst of our situation, it gives Him something to work with. That is biblical faith in action.

This is not the time to cry or whine or moan to God. From a place of peace and faith, it is time to take SPECIFIC verses that apply to your situation and pray them back to God. Then, you need to declare them boldly over the situation, so that the Lord can 'watch over' His Word to perform it in your life.

For example, if I am trusting God for physical healing for an injured bone, I might pray this way:

Father God, I thank You that you said in Your Word, "I AM the God Who heals you (Exodus15:26)," and You said of our Messiah Jesus, "...by His wounds, you are healed (Isaiah 53:5b)."

Lord, I know that you want me to be healed of this bone injury, and I thank You that Jesus bore wounds so that I could be healed. I receive Your healing power into my bones right now, in the Name of Jesus.

Bones, by the wounds that Jesus bore, you have been healed. So, be healed in the name of Jesus the Messiah!

Thank you Lord, for finishing the work that You have started in my bones. Amen.

You have to be bold, because Jesus was not wimpy when it came to dealing with sickness, demons, storms or controlling religious leaders. He spoke the Word of God, and He really let them have it!

PRAY like Jesus, and PRAISE like Jesus....

STEP 10. Praise God for a positive outcome

KEY VERSE: "Praise Him for His mighty acts; praise Him according to His excellent greatness." ~ Psalm 150:2

The Bible is a powerful book, and its Author is absolutely brilliant! In this verse, God tells you EXACTLY what to do. Once you read and memorize this verse, you can act on it day or night, no matter what situation that you are in.

"Praise Him for His mighty acts…."

You can start to thank Him for all of the great and marvelous things that He has done for you in the past, and begin to thank Him for moving in your current situation as well.

You are breathing—so praise Him. "Let everything that has breath…." He lovingly drew you to Himself—that is why you are even praying to Him or reading this book in the first place—so praise Him.

Use your brain—think of things to praise

God for, and then start to open your mouth and praise Him and thank Him for each one of them. This is a way of 'priming the pump', ie getting the praises started and flowing, until they just pour out of you like water from a water pump.

Remember, you are thanking Him for a POSITIVE OUTCOME—no matter what that outcome might be. God alone chooses who He raises from the dead, so we cannot force Him to do that.

However, we can trust Him for guidance, strength, wisdom, provision, healing, peace and all of the other benefits that He has placed in His Word for us.

If you are stuck for what to thank God for, simply start at your toes and thank Him for every part of your body, every breath that

He has given you, every meal, every friend, every good thing that has ever happened to you. That is a great place to start, if you need to prime your pump a little bit.

You should also praise God for His GREATNESS—how big and awesome and wonderful He is. No matter what happens in this current situation, you are going to praise Him with all that you have, every day, for the rest of your life—simply because He deserves your praise and worship forever.

When you have filled yourself up with praise and worship, and when you have finally gotten some sort of victory over your current situation—even if it takes weeks or months, it also puts you in a better state to be able to be a support to others. That's on the next page....

10. HELPING OTHERS WHO ARE IN A CRISIS

You are sitting in an airplane, waiting for take-off, and the cabin crew is going through the required health and safety briefing.

Little do they know that they about to teach you a vital, very scriptural lesson that you could use the rest of your life.

When they get to the portion of their

presentation where they demonstrate the oxygen masks dropping from the ceiling panel above your head, they make a very wise statement, which goes something like this:

"If you are traveling with small children or infants, make sure that you secure your own mask FIRST, before attempting to fit their masks."

It is a brilliant piece of advice. Why?

If you pass out from lack of oxygen, you will not be able to help your baby. You will not be able to help others, especially those who are vulnerable or needy.

In the same way, it is EXTREMELY IMPORTANT that you build up your own personal praise and worship life before you attempt to 'resuscitate' others—especially others who are vulnerable and are going through some type of crisis or trauma.

The reason for this is simple. People in that state of mind and emotional upheaval are more vulnerable and need careful attention. They may feel desperate, so every word counts and every action can either build them up or knock them back in a big way.

Therefore, spend the time necessary to build yourself up in your own relationship with God, as well as in your personal life of praise and worship, so that you can be better equipped to serve and help others.

That makes sense, doesn't it?

We are in the process of producing a range of resources which will help you to do just that.

The first resource that is going to help you immensely is FREE!

On the next page, I am going to give you a FREE bonus audio as a 'Thank You for purchasing this book………

FREE GIFT FOR YOU!

Thank you for purchasing this valuable book. We trust that it has been a blessing—and a vibrant introduction—into the richness of true, biblical praise and worship.

To say "Thank You" for adding this book to your collection, we want to offer you a FREE GIFT to add to your enjoyment of this book.

We have recorded a live audio with Jerry Kuzma, where he reads through parts of the text of the book and injects insightful commentary, in order to help you build a life a life full of high praises and deep worship.

You are going to thoroughly enjoy hearing from the author himself, as he draws on years of bible study, practical ministry and Godly wisdom, to share with you insights firmly based on scripture.

For a **FREE** downloadable copy of this intriguing audio, please STOP READING RIGHT NOW...and visit the webpage below...to request your copy:

<u>www.info321.com/bonus114</u>

Get your FREE bonus audio RIGHT NOW!

We will also let you know about new

releases and additional resources to help you in both your walk with the Lord and your personal and professional life.

Again, thank you for becoming our valued reader and customer, and we look forward to serving you in the future.

PLEASE POST A REVIEW!

I would really appreciate it if you could go back to the page that you purchased this book from…and leave an honest, constructive review.

(If this book has truly helped you in your praise and worship life, then please give it a 5-star rating.)

Book reviews are very important for the multitude of readers who want to know what a book is like. When readers like you post a constructive review, others get a good idea of what the book is about and how it has impacted your life.

It also gives the author some vital feedback, so that he or she can build on the positives and strengthen the areas that need it.

So, THANK YOU for posting a review!

Have a brilliant day as you praise and worship the Lord,

~ Jerry Kuzma

ABOUT THE AUTHOR

Jerry Kuzma is a publishing consultant and author, specializing in helping others to achieve expert status in their field. He and his team work with speakers, coaches, business owners and religious leaders to build their brand, expand their reach and develop passive income, along with all the financial and lifestyle benefits of the experts industry.

A polished writer and editor, Jerry is also the creator of various high-caliber multimedia products, including the "True Worship" series and the "Write Your Own Book" series.

Jerry has also been leading praise and worship in both religious and secular settings for over 25 years, from small home groups to regional conferences to government events.

He teaches and trains believers how to ignite their praise and deepen their worship in line with biblical principles.

Jerry is also available for speaking, teaching or training engagements, either in person or via the internet (so distance is no longer a limitation). Simply contact us via our support page:

www.PerissosGroup.com/support

JERRY KUZMA

ABOUT PERISSOS MEDIA

WRITE your book.
BUILD your brand.
CREATE your platform.
BROADCAST your message.
EXPAND your reach and income...

Perissos Media helps business owners, speakers, consultants, professionals, sales teams, ministry leaders and inspired individuals to PUBLISH books, audio and video training products and other marketing materials.

The goal is to BUILD your platform and ELEVATE you to Expert Status in your field—with all the financial and lifestyle benefits that come with it.

What is your passion? Are you ready to go from LOCAL to GLOBAL?

Even if you have never written a word, we have resources and services to help you get your message out, one step at a time.

For help in building or expanding your platform, and to publish your message to a greater audience, please visit:

www.IWantToPublish.com

We look forward to serving you,

Jerry Kuzma
Director
PerissosMedia.com

OTHER PRODUCTS BY PERISSOS MEDIA

True Worship vol 1: The Essence of Hebrew Worship (<u>Kindle</u> version)

Buy it now in these Amazon stores: <u>US IN UK DE FR ES IT JP BR CA MX AU</u>

True Worship vol 1: The Essence of Hebrew Worship (<u>paperback</u> version)

Amazon   UK: <u>http://www.amazon.co.uk/dp/0992667720/</u>

Amazon US: <u>http://www.amazon.com/dp/0992667720/</u>

Write Your Own Book vol 1: How to Expand Your Brand, Your Reach and Your Income

Buy it now in these Amazon stores: <u>US IN UK DE FR ES IT JP BR CA MX AU</u>

Write Your Own Book vol 2: 15 Ways to Promote Your Business, Your Message or Yourself

Buy it now in these Amazon stores: (currently in production)

Write Your Own Book...5 Minutes at a Time! (vol 3)

Buy it now in these Amazon stores: US   IN   UK   DE
FR ES IT JP BR CA MX AU

Write Your Own Book vol 4:   5 Easiest Ways to Write Your Own Book

Buy it now in these Amazon stores: US   IN   UK   DE
FR ES IT JP BR CA MX AU

Write Your Own Book…and Get More Clients! (vol 5)

Buy it now in these Amazon stores: (currently in production)

Book Impact: Seven Powerful Ways to Promote Your Business or Charity with Your Own Book

Buy it now in these Amazon stores: US   IN   UK   DE
FR ES IT JP BR CA MX AU

Music Publishing: How to Publish Your Own Music Online

Buy it now in these Amazon stores: US   IN   UK   DE
FR ES IT JP BR CA MX AU

~ ~ ~ ~ ~

For a complete and current product listing, stop reading right now and visit:

www.PerissosGroup/products

Made in the USA
Charleston, SC
11 September 2014